South Of Pittsburgh

Poems from Northern Appalachia

Michael Comiskey

Chestnut Ridge Press

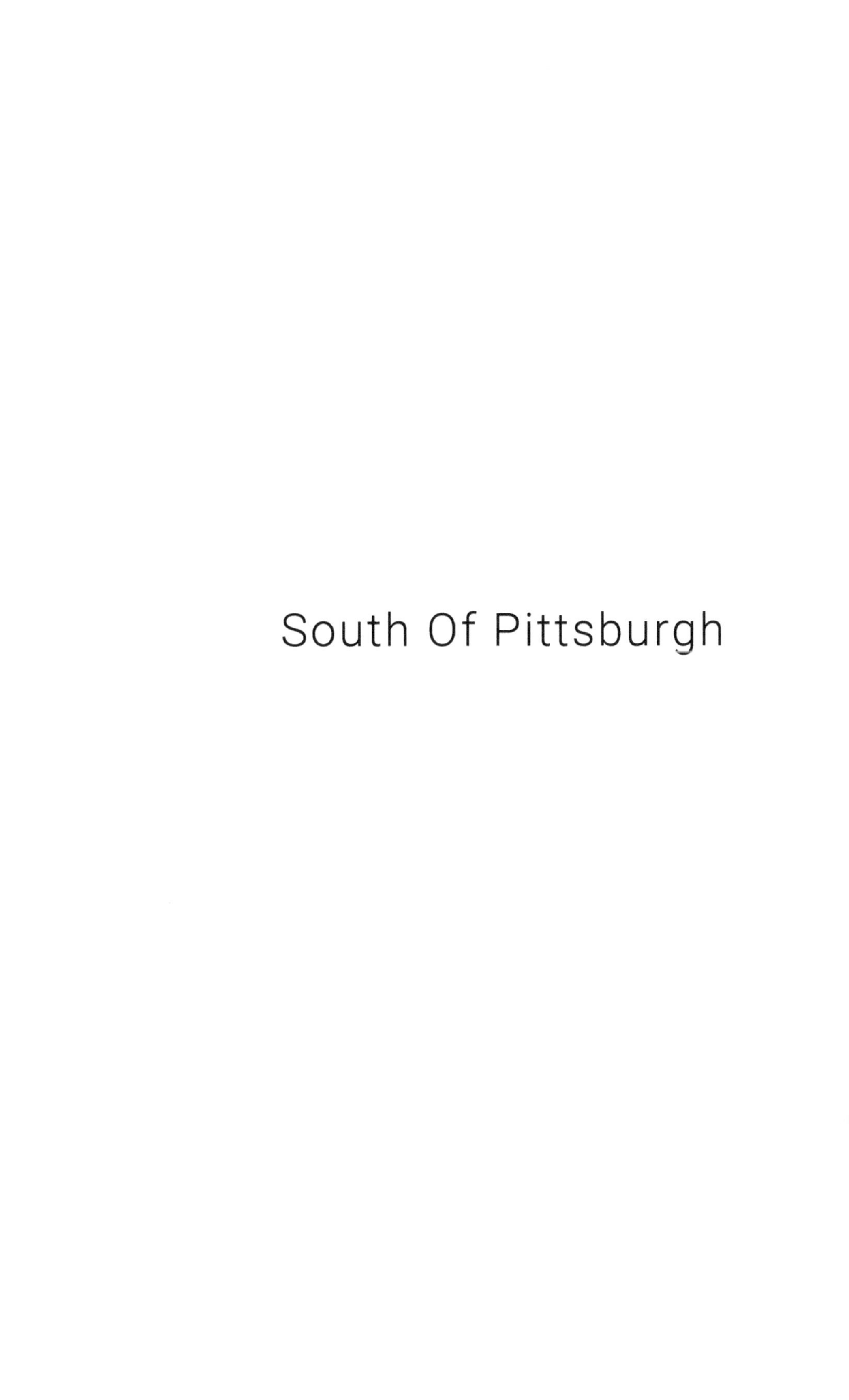

South Of Pittsburgh

First Printing, 2024

ISBN: 9798989106424

Library of Congress Control Number: 2023918386

Chestnut Ridge Press
602 East Green Street
Connellsville, Pennsylvania

Cover photo of Confluence, Pennsylvania by Greg Cromer Aerial Photography

for Mary Ann

CONTENTS

Preface

The presentation of these poems follows a seasonal theme, as the language or tone of each one suggests something seasonal.

The poems owe their genesis to my origin in a working class family of Irish and Italian descent in southwestern Pennsylvania, a region much exploited and neglected but resilient and still beautiful. They express my affectionate and, I hope, clear-eyed perspective on the rural and mountainous parts of northern Appalachia *South of Pittsburgh*.

AUTUMN

MICHAEL COMISKEY

Autumn

Those who find the winter chill adverse
might rue that time of year whose essence
is waning warmth and light, and desiccation;
yet even they applaud the transformation
of pervasive green to autumnal fluorescence—
the most scenic senescence in the universe—

and bask in the prospect of settling down
to the prescribed perfection of the year,
when all of nature resolves as it should.
And in that placid atmosphere one could
almost swear that all across the hemisphere
peace and pleasant harmony abound.

Then dying leaves engender a disquieting ferment;
the body craves a dwindling sun
that scantily suffices.
No conjured intellectual devices
thwart apprehension of a year soon done
through inescapable descent.

All those scarlet leaves turned umber
stir wistful thoughts of days gone by
when all the best tomorrows lay ahead;
and one must ask, as Hamlet: To dread
the deepening chill come nigh,
or concur in wintry slumber?

The Cash King on Route 219

Antiques! Antiques!
We Buy And Sell Everything!
Don't Need That Luggage?
We Buy From You!
We're The Cash King!

Don't Use Those Bikes?
A Clean Garage = Cash!
Guns! Guns!! Guns!!!
We Buy And Sell!
Your Source For Instant Cash!

That Dinette Set You Never Liked?
Free Appraisals @ Home!
Military Uniforms/Medals!
Clean Out Your Closet!
Cash For Your Unwanted Items!

Why Keep Unused China?
Stop And Sell!
Don't Want Those Old Rings?
We Pay U!
We're The Cash King!

Aunt Whatshername's Pin?
Cash 4 U!
Turn Your Silver Into Gold!
Stop Now!
We Pay Cash, CASH, CA$H!

We're The Cash King!

The Factory

I start my shift as jars and bottles march
in perfect ranks and columns from the oven,
glass soldiers of an army on parade.
An electric selector inspects their
warm bodies for weakness; those that don't pass
muster must be mustered out—returned to
the furnace to be melted and recast.
Maybe on their next try they can run the
obstacle course. Those that pass inspection
are packed in cartons and sent down the line.
I stack the cartons on a pallet and,
when the skid's at full strength, a forklift
whisks them to the warehouse to await
deployment to Smucker's, Kraft, or Heinz.
As I end my shift, the little troopers
still pour from the oven, and advance to be
rejected or selected, sacked or packed
for shipment. "What have I accomplished here?"
I wonder. On my next day off, I do some
shopping and I see them, gleaming in the
store light, standing tall in tight formation
on their designated shelves, in dress blues
and whites, filled with jelly or mayonnaise.
I'm proud of having done my part. Later,
I contemplate their ultimate fate: used,
recycled to form the next generation,
or buried with their fellows in a landfill.

Forgotten Places

I like forgotten places.
Where young folks leave,
though I like young folks fine;
where trains don't stop—
hell, they don't even run;
where a house is a home
and not an investment;
where people have gardens,
and chickens are "yard birds";
where you know your neighbors
because they never move
and neither will you;
where the fire department is volunteer;
where people fish;
where they sell corn by the roadside;
where they close the stores at 6
to sit on their porches
and talk of how dry it's been;
where buckwheat suppers are *haute cuisine*;
where everyone knows
everyone's mother's maiden name;
where enough is enough;
where Wal-Mart won't come;
where most Americans no longer live.

Voter Fraud

We tell you with perfect sincerity:
voter fraud is no misplaced obsession.
Our only goal is election integrity.

Corruption is a problem of great severity.
We know, because politics is our profession,
we tell you with perfect sincerity.

Sixteen Americans had the temerity
to vote twice in the presidential election!
Our only goal is election integrity.

While making voter fraud a rarity,
we'd never engage in voter suppression,
we tell you with perfect sincerity.

We'll handle the problem with utmost dexterity
and apply the most discriminating discretion.
Our only goal is election integrity.

All should agree on the following verity:
we need fair elections, that's beyond question.
We tell you with perfect sincerity:
our only goal is election integrity.

Directive at ----- University

Back out of all this now too much for us.
Personal income up thirty percent
per capita the last twenty-five years
to an all-time high for which we're grateful.
But subsidy per student has gone down
from seventy percent of total cost to ten.
Taxes must be cut. Must keep business here
without that we've no jobs for graduates.
So we and neighbor states race to bottom.
Used to be the state would promise our youth
that no one in our Commonwealth would find
they could not go to university
for lack of funds. Must cancel all that now.
Used to be that U.S. economy
served people. New directive: people serve
economy. They took the "State" out of
our name so none would think legislature
has any obligation to fund us.
Graduates earn more so let them borrow.
No mind that education serves us all.
Yeah, we shouldn't have built that climbing wall,
or built the condo-style student housing
or rehabbed the gym for fifty million.
Must do more with less: no more classes with
less than forty students. Spread word softly.

P.S. Philosophy Department must
be closed, no demand for idle thinkers.
Criminal Justice Cash Cow to be spared.

Goldenrod

Photo by Huw Williams

Ode to Goldenrod

The daffodils are crunchy memories on this
October day, illumined by your sunny plume.
And lost are lilies, violets—even the chrys-
anthemum decays. The butterflies with whom

you share rejuvenating nectars
float and flit about, refueling for migration
to Mexico. You sate the lithe collectors,
who offer you no visible appreciation.

And blooming as you do in liminal
spaces—sandlots, weedy places—unadmiring
humanity has labelled you a criminal
for inconsiderately firing

immiserating fits of cough and wheeze
until the fall's first freeze. In truth, it's ragweed,
the culprit that you bloom aside, that fills the breeze
with allergens—unlike the harmless seed

that you obligingly transmit by bees and birds.
Oh, goldenrod, you've been so carefully conceived
to benefit both man and beast, and yet no kindly words
you'll hear—so sunlike and so misperceived.

The Amish Way

Shall we admire those strangers in our midst?
Fair and true in all relations, Godly
in all things, no harm they do another.
And they live by this cobwebbed commandment:
"But I say unto you that you resist
not evil. But whosoever smite thee
on thy right cheek, turn to him the other."

And if you ask: "Does nonresistance spur
the criminal?" they might well ask of you,
"Who more powerful ever lived than He,
who cognizant of death, observed divine intent
and freely gave Himself to suffer?"
"You have no fear," you ask, "of those who'll
come for you all?" They might cite history

and reply, "Did not the Romans try that?"
If you point to differences from then,
and the criminal talents of today's
regimes, they'll tell you their one commitment
is reaching the City of God—by that
they disregard the soiled city of men.
And there is where we go our separate ways.

The Apples

I hadn't set out to find apples that fall—
on a mountain road I made my passage
to partake of Appalachia's fabled foliage.
By a van on the roadside sat a man in overalls
and straw hat. On the van a handsome sign
read, "Apples 25 cents, $2 for nine."
You know, I haven't had a fresh-picked apple
since I don't know when, I thought.
For just two bucks, that's certainly a lot
of apples; on the price I wouldn't cavil
with the man, whose face betrayed a frown
there on that roadway miles from town.
I began to wonder what variety
of apples the forlorn farmer sold—
Braeburn, Fuji, Gala, Red or Golden
Delicious? I hoped, but only silently,
a farmer in these ancient mountains
might produce my favorite: Jonathans.
Having forgotten all thought of leaf-peeping,
my synapses were flush
with dreams of all the luscious stuff
I'd cook. My heart was leaping
with visions of tarts and pies I could bake,
and cobblers and turnovers I would make—
all loaded with cinnamon, my favorite spice.
Or I'd slice them and pair them with Riesling
—a dry Chardonnay would also be pleasing—
and Julienned slices with cheese would be nice.
For humans, the apple has infinite uses—
raw, baked, cooked, or pressed for its juices.

So not much farther down that road
I pulled the car over and made a U-turn,
and back to the man with the van I returned.
Then up to the farmer I eagerly strode:
"I see you've got apples, two dollars for nine."
"No sir," he smiled, "I'm selling signs."

Volunteer Firefighters

To a sophisticated friend I sang
my praises for volunteer firemen
"who will come to your house at 3 AM
to fight a fire." "Oh," my savvy friend
replied, "they're just big macho boys
who parade in big red fire truck toys."

Well, call me a fool.
But the nearest paid fire department
is 24 miles from my house.
And lots of boys work with big toys:
railroaders, airline pilots, auto mechanics,
and excavators, just to name a few.

But they won't:

Put out fires;
Save you from a flood and
then pump out your basement;
Cordon off downed wires;
Rescue people from ravines;
Free you from your wrecked car;
Save a child who's fallen down a well;
Stand on dark roads in dark coats
to slow traffic at accident scenes;
Recover drowning victims;
Search for lost children, hikers,
bikers, and nursing home residents;
Clean up a chemical spill;
or fetch your cat from a treetop.

Not to mention saving
some stupid, ungrateful animal
likely to bite or gore them
that's stuck down a storm sewer
or out on the ice.
That's in addition to training, training, training.

On Saturdays they sacrifice
their time selling hoagies
or holding an empty boot
and looking mournfully at you,
hoping you'll donate loose change;
or cooking at the pancake supper,
or cleaning the fire hall after a wedding.
Or they're working bingo on Thursday night,
or selling chances on big screen TVs,
or holding the annual township fair.
All to raise bucks for their half-million dollar
pumper trucks or their million-dollar ladder truck
or other stuff so they can fight fires
and do—for you
and me—
all the things
in the previous verse.
For free.

Most of them weren't the "smart kids"
who went to college as you and I did.
So if they parade in big red trucks
and toot their own air horns,
and march in white-gloved,
puffy-chested, beer-bellied unison

on Memorial Day,
I say God bless them.

The Carnegie Free Library

Built atop a relocated graveyard
and acknowledged to be haunted,
the sandstone structure's stood since 1900.

You open the heavy outer door
and plunge into *eau de senescence*,
like the fusty sanctuary of an antique church.

You wonder if it always felt like this,
or how long it took before it felt this way.
Perhaps you're here because

you're living in your car,
or you need someone to talk to,
however softly, or you need to walk more,

and there's no better place to walk to.
Or you can't pay your heating bill
and you need to warm up.

Or maybe you've come to resume an acquaintance
with Jane Austen, or renew a friendship
with a classmate in the corner café,

where you can get panini, tea, or coffee,
and a bowl of creamy potato, basil and tomato,
or butternut squash soup.

Perhaps you've come to get a copy
of your favorite author's latest book—
the one the librarian is holding for you,

or you're examining the other book
in the "New Titles" section.
Or you're just being practical and you've come

to read a free copy of *Consumer Reports*,
Good Housekeeping, or *Family Handyman*.
Perhaps you've wandered to the reference section,

and you're engrossed in *The International Dictionary
    of Thoughts*
or *The Encyclopedia of Mystery and Detection*.
Or you're comfortably lodged in the cushy green chair

in the corner of the Reading Room,
and you're browsing biographies of Jimmy Stewart,
Mr. Rogers, Charles Schulz, and Dolly Parton.

(You used to value Dolly for her foremost assets,
but now you just plain like the gal.)
Before you leave, you walk

to the circular circulation desk
and use the chip-equipped descendant of your
first-ever library card to check out a book;

the visage of Andrew Carnegie looks down
from the wall and approves.
And as you leave this haunted house of books

atop the former cemetery, you almost hope
to glimpse the ghost
of some Victorian dressmaker

the exhumers left behind,
or a desiccated librarian with a bony finger
raised to her missing lips,

or the sylph-like image
of your six-year old self,
flitting among the stacks.

The Windmills of West Virginia

In northern West Virginia countless coal mines
hollowed out the mountains and the hills.
The old techniques of mining have wreaked
havoc with the native creeks and streams;
some of them flow orange to this day.
Then mountaintops were blown away
to bare the highest, thinnest seams
of coal beneath the mountains' peaks.
Plantations of immense white windmills
dominate the ravaged ridges' spines.

Some top out at four hundred feet high!
On Mt. Storm a hundred thirty turbines stretch
twelve miles on a ridge and power sixty thousand
homes. To some the waving windmills range
like giant crosses in a winking, blinking cemetery.
Others see the white behemoths as necessary
progress in the war on climate change.
But windmills speak. Some there on the mountain
swear a simple *swoosh* is all they catch;
others claim the rush of air evokes an endless sigh.

The Ballad of Betty Knox

In the Allegheny mountains
from roughly Dunbar to Ohiopyle,
lies a dark and rugged region—
a hundred square miles

of cliff-crested ridges and forest so thick
you can't see a bear at twenty yards.
Only the most hardy ever lived there:
in the 1800s, life was hard

for the mountain folk, who eked a livin'
raisin' cattle, buckwheat, corn, and rye
and cuttin' timber on the rocky slopes.
Not a soul alive today knows why

they came or stayed. You're probably not surprised
to learn that in that coarse environment
the mountaineers told stories 'round their fires—
it was their only source of entertainment.

A lot of those tales were tall ones,
I'll admit, and most are long forgotten.
But there's one such tale that's never died—
and that's because it was begotten

of the truth—and that would be the legend
of Betty Knox. She was born in 1842
on a farm at Kentuck Knob. Early death
come often then, and when she was but two

years old, her mother died,
leavin' little Betty all alone
for raisin' by her pap. But she grew up
and helped him with plantin' and hoin'

and clearin' new fields, and cuttin'
trees for buildin' and burnin',
just as if she was a son.
That's in addition to cookin'

and keepin' house—or cabin in their case.
Yes, Betty was a strong young miss,
a girl of great beauty, some say.
But I wouldn't credit this

part of the story too much
because it can't be verified—
you know how people add to stories.
Well, when she was 17, her father died

in a logging accident. And she buried him
beneath a spreading maple tree
on Kentuck Knob. You'd think
a girl alone up there would move, but Betty

was no ordinary girl. She kep' on
farmin' and workin' the land,
haulin' water and cuttin' timber
just as good as any man.

She even took a new line
for herself: Betty had an ox named,
um, I forget what, but her and the ox
hauled other farmers' grain

out of the mountains and down the slopes
and over the creeks and hills
to a place outside o' Dunbar
called Ferguson's Mill.

She'd begin each trip at daybreak
and then return by night
with 15 sacks of flour on the ox.
And what a welcome sight

that was to her strugglin' neighbors.
Soon, she'd cleared a well-worn way
for 13 miles through forest and rocks—
you can still see that path today:

if you follow Dunbar Creek
for five miles up from town,
you'll see where Betty crossed
that stream. And if you look around

the hillside to the south,
you'll see a spring lined with stone
that Betty put there like she done
everything—all alone.

Hunters and hikers still use it today.
Well, come the fall of 1862,
Betty found a wounded Union soldier
on her path. And Betty, a true

Free-Soiler, took him to her cabin,
where she did her best to care
for 'im. (He'd been wounded
in West Virginia, and scared

of army doctors, he'd deserted.)
But no matter how hard Betty tried,
his condition gradually worsened,
and in the spring of 1863 he died.

And Betty, heartbroken,
buried him beside her pap on
Kentuck Knob. My granddad
claimed he had a map on

which the graves were shown,
but he died before I ever saw it.
So Betty went back to the dreary
work of farmin' and all it

took to make a livin' there,
includin' the haulin' of grain
and flour for her neighbors
(a relative term in the mountains

where people lived so far apart).
Betty was quiet but much respected
by the mountain folk
and by the mill hands who expected

her arrival every week in harvest time.
But suddenly, in the fall of 1868,
she vanished. Search teams went out
along her weekly route, but none could locate

the missing woman or her ox.
And that's the way things stayed
until the following spring, when children
playin' on Betty's route made

a terrible discovery in the woods:
chained to a tree
was the skeleton of an ox
the same size as Betty's.

The strangest thing about it was
the place they found the beast, for
that very spot had been the center
of the search just months before.

And there was somethin' else:
Betty Knox was never known
to use a chain to lead her ox,
and thus the chain was not her own.

There's been speculation ever since
about whose ox it was, and why
a man would chain an ox
like that and let it die.

If it was a joke, we still don't
know what happened to
poor Betty. And if it weren't no joke,
why would her killer leave a clue

there in the forest?
You can see now why this mystery
has roiled Fayette County ever since.
And if you doubt this history

ask someone from Dunbar, or take
that road that Betty built for her and her ox
and sit where it fords Dunbar Creek
among the virgin hemlocks.

Find the spring still lined with stone
and sit there on the rocks.
And you may hear a man's voice whisper,
Betty Knox, Betty Knox.

Shanksville

One if by land, two if by sea.
And patriots came.
Then three if by air,
and patriots were there.
Just listen to their names:
Cushing, Garcia, Glick and Bay,
Homer, Felt, Corrigan, DeLuca.
Over the towers of Pittsburgh they flew
on a bright, sunny day.
And then they joined the fight:
Gronlund, Beamer, Talignani and Nacke,
Guadagno, Martinez, Bingham, Burnett.

The world will little note,
nor long remember, what I write.
But go to Shanksville—
on the wall, read each name,
and you'll never forget
that patriots came.

For a complete list of the passengers
and crew on Flight 93, visit
https://www.flight93friends.org/flight-93-
passengers-crew.

WINTER

Winter

Summer's steamy languor
and the slow decay of fall
make us covet sweet repose,
and seek to do as nature does
—or seems to do—
and slumber through
the wintry night
till joyous spring awakes us.

But humans, unlike others,
have much to do in wintertime,
must venture out in grudging light
and frigid clime.

And when I do,
I'm forcibly revived
as winter stings my cheeks
and nose, and pierces hide
and nearly bone—
and fallen snow
bedazzles with such
brilliance as a million
tiny jewels,
so charming to the eye
but cruel
to the touch.

Perhaps it's just in memory
that winter seems so bracing,
that icy tingle feels refreshing

only when it's ending—
when back inside I'm facing
out my window as blowing snow,
descending from the eaves,
veils winter's wanton temper.

Monongahela Valley

Mills and coke works lined the river
from Pittsburgh to Monessen.
We was the city that didn't sleep—
it was dark in the day and light in the night.
The mill whistle blew at seven, three, and eleven.
But now the only whistle in this Valley
is the cry of the wind.

The union couldn't do nothin',
and the politicians wouldn't. The gains
from trade must of went somewhere else,
'cause all we got here was the pain.
We all hoped steel would come back like before.
But when they shut the last furnace,
I didn't need no raven to tell me No More.

The G20 come to Pittsburgh, and met
in shiny corporate castles downtown,
to show the world how an old
steel town could bounce back.
They didn't come to Braddock or Duquesne,
where the jobs went out and the heroin come in,
and now the only whistle is the cry of the wind.

I was gonna retire at fifty-five.
They laid me off at fifty-three.
The government lady said
Go To School and You'll Retool!
But computers and nursing wasn't for me.
At least in the mill you made good money,
but I don't need no raven to tell me No More.

Now I sell stuff at Best Buy on commission.
My wife cleans a doctor's office at night.
I told my boys they had to go.
One's a teacher in Texas,
the other deals cards at an Indian casino.
I'd love to have 'em back again.
But I don't need no raven to tell me No More,
'cause now the only whistle in this Valley
is the cry of the wind.

The Maple Trees

To noble maple trees that stand astride
the laureled ridges, humans come in dark
of wintertime. They pierce the shaggy bark
with steel and pray the maple gods provide
their yearly crop of maple nectars.
The trees, which use the liquids as a kind
of blood, don't seem to mind:
they satisfy the happy collectors.
The sturdy trees, unharmed by human tap,
distill their juice from water and sun,
and yield a dozen gallons from each one.
But for humans lacking that sweet sap,
a waffle would be dry and awful,
nor would any naked flapjack flap.

The Wild Turkey

One chilly, early winter's day,
a dark and brooding, oblong figure stood
between my garden and the naked wood,
seeming headless as it hunched the other way.
What it was, I wished I didn't know.
In truth, I knew at once it had to be
an injured wild turkey. I could plainly see
it stood on just one foot, and so
the other dangled useless in the air.
In order to find enough to eat,
a turkey scratches the ground with her feet—
her, because she bore no turkey tassel there.
Abandoned by her brood, she combed the snow
in filaments with her slender, pointed beak,
a lame and ineffectual technique
sure to lead to death both cruel and slow.
Informed that there was little possibility
of treatment for the wounded bird,
her pitiful condition stirred
me to assist her in her disability.
Behind my house I threw some seed;
staying far from her as best I could,
she nonetheless flew to the darkling wood.
In her absence, squirrels ate all her feed.
I'd also hoped that I could teach her
that my presence in the yard meant food.
When she hopped away, I had to conclude
my teaching hadn't reached her.
Another problem was the bird's old brood:
they'd show up every now and then

and push aside the crippled hen,
and then eat all of her intended food.
From the birds' perspective, that made sense:
to sustain the species they don't need her,
and thus, to them, it's senseless to feed her;
injured birds receive no recompense.
And were the crippled hen to mate, then
she'd not be able to scratch the earth
and dig a nest, as turkeys do, to birth
her eggs and incubate them.
And any chicks in a brood
of hers would very likely die.
She couldn't walk, and they couldn't fly:
she couldn't lead her young to food.
On Christmas Day I put feed in the yard,
having failed again to entreat
the bird. As if to make my failure complete,
it began to snow unusually hard.
As snowflakes covered the corn I'd spread,
I cursed in true King Lear-like form
at all that conspired, including this storm,
to leave the wounded turkey dead.
After late December, I saw no more her
labored lurching. Only in a human thought
she moves, and does a sprightly turkey trot,
freed from nature's savage order.

Forgotten

People in this region feel forgot.
And well they ought,
sacrificed to doctrines misbegot.

"Clean and Green With New Technologies"

Big Morgan Mountain stood three hundred
      million years,
and saw a thousand ice sheets come and go.
Its slopes held hardwoods nine flights high.

They stripped the trees first.
Then four hundred foot
of mountaintop
—*overburden*—
was blown through the air
and dumped in the hollows.
A dragline cut 29 inches of
clean coal
from the carcass.

Now a grey stump
two miles square
greets the eye.
An earth and slate dam,
with its deepening pool
of black, sulfurous
coal-wash water looms
above the valley.
In castrate hollows
seep orange, oozy eddies
of iron pyrite—
fool's gold.

But who is the fool?
And who has the gold?

Nothing can live
in the alkaline soil.
A Mars lander could come here
and not know the difference,
except for the Astroturf softball fields
shown on TV.

You know the ones—
they're lighted at night.

The White

Silently the dusty white descends
on every hill and valley
south of Pittsburgh,
muffling the senses.
Neither town nor country can escape.
The powdery patina
crushes everything it touches.

Family Graves

Some bond of blood or intellect compels
my pilgrimage to Old Saint Joseph's Cemetery,
where interments ceased in 1983.
I visit long-dead family, their name misspelled
forever on their marble slab, set in the earth
on the verge of the graveyard's overgrown section,
whose stones comprise a barely visible collection
of shattered, sunken shards, the dates of birth,
and death, and names effaced. No one breathing
now knew any of my family buried there;
all that has survived of them are scant bare
facts and tantalizing legends wreathing
them in mystery. Why did my great-granddad's clan
leave County Monaghan? Were they horse thieves
as per family lore? Or, as some believe,
troublesome Irish republicans?
And what to make of my great-grandmother,
who with her sister left County Meath,
and having put one husband beneath
the sod, married her dead husband's brother?
Did my father's Uncle Jimmy really jump
into the river to escape the law?
(That was the last the family ever saw
him.) Then there's Dad's Aunt Mary, called Stump
because she only had one leg. What kind of life
did she lead in that charming milieu?
Her brother Bernard was one-legged, too.
Why did he and three brothers have no wife
or children? Bernard at least had a usable craft:
an experienced B&O Railroad machinist,

he made his own aluminum prosthesis.
It stood in the attic long after
he died. Advanced for its time,
it was fully adjustable,
and made of an alloy, almost indestructible.
Gone to a scrap heap, its loss was a crime.
And last there's Daddy's Uncle Arthur.
Returning from the Great War he
told darkly entertaining stories.
Ordered by his colonel to fetch some water,
"Sir, I'm not a bit thirsty," he said.
But he got the water—in no great hurry.
And when he finally returned he
found the colonel and his retinue dead.

If the dead live in our memories,
what happens to them when we die?
Very few will be remembered by
the Muse of history.
However endearing their stories to me,
with each passing year
the brambles creep nearer
in the family cemetery.

Elegy for Pinkerton Hill

A mountain stood between points A and B.
The tunnel that had served a century
no longer served—it wasn't large enough
for newer, taller freight cars packed with stuff
from China. So the mountain had to go,
an impediment to the faster flow
of flip-flops, swimsuits, chaise chairs—
a potpourri of happy household wares,
all very slightly cheaper than before.
Now a gash three hundred feet deep and four
hundred feet wide forms a permanent scar
on the ridge—but handles larger freight cars.
The gouging added to our GDP
and nudged up labor productivity—
output's up a one-time .01 percent;
productivity leaped the same extent.
These statistics do not count the cost
of a mountain sundered, forever lost.

I Live Alone

The furnace turns on, the furnace turns off.
The furnace turns on, the furnace turns off.
The furnace is my friend.

Only the Name Has Been Changed

Trey Ballentine's obituary ran
last Tuesday, victim of a highway crash,
16. The driver of the car in which
he rode, 19, was badly hurt. They wore
no seatbelts and were traveling at what
the state police called an "excessive speed."
Trey and four siblings had three different
surnames among them. He was living with
an aunt and uncle just before he died.
He loved to ride his dirt bike in the woods.
His funeral procession was a long
one—more than 50 cars. So many cared.
His coffin was borne by his truck. His truck.
Another truck, a pickup, bore his bike.

Fracked

Green machines resembling robots populate
the farms and fields outside of Pittsburgh.
They suck up natural gas from strata eight
thousand feet down.

The wells were "fracked"—
drilled and then injected with fluids
under pressure, so they cracked
the Earth and left the gas to flow.

A helpful web site says those fluids
are composed of mostly sand and water—
benzene and ammonia are also included
and common chemicals in consumer goods

and the food we eat, just
like the arsenic and formaldehyde
you add to your breakfast
cereal every morning.

One drilling pad might
host some 40 wells and use 8,000 tons
of chemicals per site.
The helpful web page doesn't tell you

that some of this stew is ejected
from the well when pumping ceases.
But not to worry—the quantity rejected
is only moderately radioactive.

It's stored in open pits until it's evacuated
by truck to make the Earth puke
somewhere else—it may even evaporate
harmlessly into the air.

Thus radionuclides and chlorides
erupting from punctures in the Earth
may safely be neutralized by bromides
spewing from the corner office.

Or the brew is taken
down a deep well in Ohio, where the
slippery goo facilitates the quaking
of the Earth.

These earthquakes occur around Dayton
and Cleveland, in the main.
But they could use some shakin'
and updatin' anyway.

When the flow of gas slows,
a well can be abandoned or be
fracked again. But no
abandoned wells are here—

the companies just designate
them as "idle";
by that means they vitiate
the law that says abandoned wells

must be plugged up with cement.
So drillers may return to drill again.
And if they don't, they circumvent
the need to plug the well—

as well as to restore the contours
of the ground around the site.
We've seen this film before:
with the mines that foul our waters.

The drillers will go out of business,
and when the wells deteriorate,
the public will inherit the mess.
We in Appalachia don't attach a

lot of faith to pledged protections:
drillers pay a bond to cover future plugs
and restorations, but collections
are too low to cover future costs.

In the meantime, though, the gush of gas
has cut its price, encouraging consumption.
I've even got a free pass
from the well outside my house:

I get free gas from my cold water tap.
I just run a hose from my sink to my stove—
and I'm cookin' with gas! And the crap
that burning gas puts in the atmosphere

is only half as bad as coal.
But it'll still be hot as hell someday—the fact
is, gas grants us just a short parole.
Let's face the fact: we're fracked.

The Dinosaurs of the Mid-Atlantic

The dinosaurs of Pennsylvania,
Maryland, and West Virginia
show themselves in winter mainly.
They slide down snowy slopes
on skis and boards
in Poconos and Alleghenies.
They do not see, nor
do they hear, the meteor.
But they can feel it in their bones.

Evelyn
1947-2020

A flower grew in Harlan,
a precious, fragile sort.
The gardeners, a man and woman,
knew not how to care for it.

The flower blossomed nonetheless:
the leaves and petals, once unfurled,
released exquisite radiance
upon a too prosaic world.

Early frosts beset the flower,
or maybe just some normal frosts.
The flower lacked the power
to withstand them and was lost.

Bypassed

It's official: Dunnville has been bypassed.
The politicians cut the ribbon on
the ribbon of new highway yesterday.
The two-lane road went around the mountains;
the new road has been blasted through them,
costing thirty million dollars per mile.
At every turn rock faces face us.
But benefits outweigh the short-term costs:
the six million dollar cost-benefit
analysis has said it would be so.
(Aren't all of these analyses the same?
Why couldn't we just pay six million bucks
for one and get the others all for free—
just change the route number and the town name?)
We're told our highways must connect to
other highways. It simply wouldn't do
to build just a few. So now you can shave
thirty seconds off your trip from Dunnville
to Cumberland or Pittsburgh. Truckers save
a good deal more than that: trucks from FedEx,
UPS, and Amazon now bypass
bypassed Dunnville 'round the clock on the new
Dunnville Bypass—no need to go through town.

There's a new Flying-J on the highway.
But the bypassed denizens of Dunnville
commonly call it the new Flying-F.
There you'll find car washes, waxes, faxes,
oil changes, money transfers out of town,
and H and R Block to do your taxes

on all the wages you'll make working there.
Death knell to most of the restaurants in town,
it features KFC and Taco Bell
and Subway and a Cinnabon restaurant
where you can get a fresh breakfast croissant
and another for the road. Coffee fans
can choose from latte, mocha, decaf, caf,
cappuccino or espresso. Creamers
featured there are Caramel Macchiato,
Mocha Mudslide, Coconut Collagen,
Himalayan Salted Caramel, Mushroom,
Cinnamon Roll, the ever-essential
Omega Power Creamer Vanilla
with Grassfed Ghee, Macadamia Fudge,
Turmeric, Keto Bomb, and Toffeenut.
There's one for every coffee nut you know.

Down on Center Street, decreasing numbers
of people and cars disturb Dunnville's peace.
The town's now a bedroom community,
but none can say to where—a bystander
to the march of impoverishing progress.
Out on the highway, the UPS and
the Amazon trucks pass by night and day.
The Flying-J is open twenty-four
seven, while the rest of Dunnville slumbers.

Elegy for Jeffrey
1958-2021

Jeffrey's obit ran online on Monday.
Two paragraphs, it ran just one day.
Survivors were his dog and brother Lee.
After school he joined the U.S. Army
and came back to work construction
as a "laborer." Multiple obstructions
in his shoulders—"impingement syndrome"—
rendered him unable to drive home
from work; he spent his last years on SSDI.
On a thousand a month, he couldn't get by,
and then he took jobs working under the table—
handy work when his shoulders were able.
So welcome to the U.S. working class,
where by sixty-three you can kiss your ass
goodbye in our kinder, gentler nation.
There are millions of Jeffreys in his generation.
Scholars have noted their characteristics;
they'll offer you mountains of dismal statistics
on job loss, disability, self-medication,
and personal and family disintegration.
See them yourself in a working class town:
go to a diner and just look around.
Gaunt or obese, the grey quotidian
shuffles by on its way to oblivion.

The Burned-Over District

He will rise! He will come again!
He Won! He was Betrayed!
Fuck Biden! Let's Go Brandon!

say the jarring signs that line the roadsides
and the banners draping modest houses
outside Pittsburgh. Every day I see them,
but I couldn't help, as I made my way
down the Alleghenies, to a conference
held in Carolina, to wonder why
the people behold Him with such fervor
as they once reserved for the Risen Lord.
At noon I stopped at Kate's Café and took
a counter seat. A TV on the wall
blasted Fox News's "Outnumbered" program.
A man in blue suit, white shirt and red tie
spoke in dark terms of people voting twice
in Arizona and Pennsylvania,
specifically in the big cities there.
WIDESPREAD VOTER FRAUD REPORTED
ran the banner on the bottom of the screen.

"Well, I'm not surprised. That's Philadelphia
for ya," said Bob on my left. (I could see
the name "Bob" on his shirt, along with an
emblem for "Johnny Whittaker's Lawn Care.")
"I'm not surprised at all. I wouldn't put
it past 'em." As I sought not to argue
but to understand my compatriot,
who seemed of a type most confused to me,

I said—or lied—"You know, up Pittsburgh way
where I come from, the people are pretty
much for Biden"—a lie, again, as I
live in the country, not in the city.
"Why is Trump so very popular here?"
He looked me over with a wary eye
and firmly replied, "Because he tells it
like it is—no political bullshit."
The *Washington Post* had calculated
that President Trump prevaricated
thirty thousand times while in the White House,
and I trusted that enumeration,
but I didn't say that and let it pass—
I knew that Bob was sure to disagree.
"Could you give me an example?" I asked.
"He tells it like it is about just what?"
"Well," he said, "like all this foreign trade shit.
The Silverex plant that made car paint here,
they told us either we agreed to cut
our pay and benefits or else they'd move
the plant to Mexico. But we said NO
and off they went. And now there's no jobs here.
It was Clinton and Gore that left 'em go,
with their goddam NAFTA. Know what I mean?"
As someone who'd long taught economics,
I thought of my longtime econ textbooks;
they said workers in high-wage nations lose,
while capital wins, from opening trade.
Guess that happened here.
But they also claimed the "losers" from trade—
collateral damage, you might call them—

could be compensated by trade's "winners."
Guess that didn't happen here.
"And then they get me comin' and goin'.
Just in case I can still make a living,
they let in immigrants from Mexico.
Our jobs went there, and their people come here."
Smelling something suspicious in that speech,
I asked him what was wrong with Mexicans.
"They cut my wages—they'll work for nothing.
I'm so tired of hearing people saying,
'Supply and demand, supply and demand'—
sets the price of everything, they say.
What about the supply and demand for *me*?
What about *my* wages? If you have more
people comin' in to take jobs like mine,
don't that cut *my* wages? Why don't supply
and demand apply to *me* and *my* wage?"
I thought about those old textbooks again:
supply and demand was gospel in them.
They also said that immigrants expand
employment opportunities for all—
migrants don't take jobs from the native-born.
But Bob was making a different point—
other things equal, more unskilled labor
means lower wages for unskilled labor.
And then the books said that workers like Bob
could go to retraining for higher-skill jobs.
Guess that didn't happen here, either.
That's when Bob left to cut somebody's grass.

"And they're fine with killin' babies, too," said
Sarah to my right. "It's against God's law

to kill that little baby in your womb.”
Startled, I didn’t know how to respond.
But then I thought of a paper I’d read
in a college philosophy class—
in it a famous philosopher made
a case favoring legal abortion.
I thought twice and thrice before I sprang it
on Sarah, someone sitting next to me
in Kate’s nondescript Café. The subject
was incendiary, and what difference
did it make if she agreed or not
with me or the famous philosopher?
I still don’t know why, but I took the plunge:
“Some believe the unborn is a person
that deserves protection, and some do not.
But suppose you wake up in the morning
to find a perfect stranger tied to you,
let’s say a musician, forty years old,
without a kidney. Now, he’s certainly
a person. Should you be required by law
to let him use your kidneys, tied to you,
to keep him alive? After all, we don’t
require other people to do things like
that to keep others alive. You don’t have
to risk your life to save a drowning man.”
“How the hell did he get into my bed?”
she asked. “Oh, that doesn’t matter,” I said,
“the question is whether you should be made
to lend your body to save another.”
“Well,” she replied, “I’ve had a child, a girl,
and I didn’t feel she was no stranger
when she was growin’ in me.” “But should you

be required by the government to let
another person seize your body to
sustain his life?" "Well, in the case of the
music man, mebbe not, 'cause he needs me
for the next forty years, and God knows I've
got other things to do. But by the time
I find out that I'm pregnant, my baby
only needs me for the next seven months,
and then she might live ninety years or more.
So I'd be awful hard put to favor
myself in that situation, ya know?"
"But what if you couldn't care for the child?"
I asked. "Well then I shouldn't have made her,
and besides, I got family what could
care for 'er. Or maybe I'd give 'er up
for adoption to a family that can't
make their own baby. Now mister, that'd
be real hard for me to do, ya know, but
I wouldn't take her ninety years from 'er
to save myself seven months o' burden."
I thought of asking her whether she thought
that all other women should have to see
things in that light. But I saw no point in
pressing; I sought no victory over her.

I finished the breakfast I'd ordered for lunch,
which cost me $6.99. As I left,
I wished Sarah well and left Kate's behind.
But they've been on my mind, Bob and Sarah.
We might have touched on some other topics.
What good would those discussions there have done?
I hope it's gone alright for them, but I

can't help thinking that on their good shoulders
the rough beast slouched again toward Washington.

SPRING

Witching Spring

After months of frost and ice,
Spring fills my heart with frothy hope
that she and I might soon elope
to summer's balmy paradise.
But angered to be seen an in-between,
a mere liaison, Spring demands respect
as no less pleasing, no less perfect,
if a princess to Summer's sultry queen;
and chastens with a tart reprise
of winter, till sufficiently appeased
by pleadings of appreciation
for her tender virtues, she surrenders
warmth, resurgent life, and restoration
of her witching vernal splendors.

Mountains

So close to Heaven
Stone cathedrals where we go
to lift our spirit

The Jews of Appalachia

No one knows precisely why they came here.
The early Jews of Appalachia, long since passed,
had motives known to God but lost to history.
Perhaps it should be no surprise or mystery,
though, that people so long shunned and outcast
landed here after wandering two thousand years:
this outcast region offered opportunities
presented by the region's major industries.
But, as elsewhere, finding few unprejudiced
employers, these itinerants, these dispossessed,
began their own establishments, little companies
that served their little prosperous communities.
They built and tended well-kept homes
and greatly prized hard work and education,
obeyed the law and paid their taxes.
As we all know, though, the fact is
they achieved despite genteel discrimination,
yet wished their neighbors undisturbed *shalom*.
Dispersed again now are the Sterns and Greensteins,
not by wind or edict but by shuttered mills and mines.
They've left behind born-again Churches of God
with six-pointed stars on their white-washed facades.

The Trout Lily

Photo from pxfuel.com

Ode to Trout Lilies

"Consider the lilies of the field,
how they grow; they toil not,
neither do they spin: And yet I say
unto you, That even Solomon
in all his glory was not arrayed
like one of these."

From the Sermon on the Mount
(Matthew 6:27-28)
King James Version

Consider eastern Erythronium,
known better as the yellow trout lily.
It thrusts up leaf-like cotyledons
in the spring—lancelike, smooth, elliptical—
of purplish puce and waxen green.
Atop the stem the perigoneum
reclines as if asleep, its solitary
flower blooming once in seven seasons.
Bright canary-hued, the tepals—petals—
flair toward earth and flex aloft, their sheen

a beacon in the forest; the pendent
pistil and the purple stamens cling
to slender filaments and seem suspended
in mid-air. Almost incomparably shy,
the precious flower blooms a fortnight
after winter. Utterly dependent
on the pallid sun of early spring,
its transitory tenancy is ended

not by hungry herbivores, but high,
exfoliating oaks that hoard the light.

The lily's speckled leaves resemble so
a trout that Indians believed it meant
a blooming lily signaled time for us
to fish. One wouldn't dream that random plants
and animals would closely synchronize,
as few would deem a flower would grow
in such a cold and dim environment.
The lily, though, is *myrmecochorous*—
its fruit is food for colonies of ants;
thus plant and ant—not fish—do synergize.

As for ants, they have no wish to nurture
lily flowers, nor the flowers to assist
the ants, who take the fragile flower's fruit
to feed their young in subterranean nests.
But bratty ants won't eat the seeds therein,
and thus begins a paradigm of Mother Nature's
celebrated skill at symbiosis:
lily seeds in anty refuse heaps take root.
And thus the dainty lily thrives in forests
cool and dim; it toils not, nor does it spin.

Appalachian River

She starts her journey high
upon an Appalachian mountain;
Always starting, never ending,
Flow on, Youghiogheny

First a trickle, then a stream,
down cascades none has ever seen,
with gentle fury tumbling down
Go on, Mama Yough

Northward going, swiftly flowing
waters gather strength;
A writhing river loosed on hapless nature
goes her way

Mountains rise to block her path
and useless will they be;
Not faith alone moves mountains—
Flow on, mighty Yough

Through Laurel Hill and Chestnut Ridge
and gorge and gashes she has cut
with rapier-like white waters

Beguiling beauty beckons you to enter her—
    Beware!
She takes you swiftly in her arms
and carries you you know not where

At last she's into gentler lands
where once were towering ranges,

cut down to size by a diamond
we call
Youghiogheny

Rain Watchers

I watched in the dark as a thundercloud burst
on the oaks and the sycamores outside my house,
their leaves in great billows against the night sky.
I opened the sash, and their *sh- sh- sh-* shimmering
sound filled the air.

My father and grandfather always watched rain.
Why do we share such a curious trait?
Did all of our ancestors watch the rain, too—
in Ireland, where rain meant they'd eat a while more?
'Tis a wonder indeed that water—*Water*—
should fall from the sky.

Fallingwater

The architect of Fallingwater, Mister Frank Lloyd Wright,
thrust up a labyrinth projecting
terraces and columns in the air—
they float atop a cataract.
A cantilever counteracts
the strain of nature's forces there,
producing intersecting
sentiments of tension and delight.

The hovering house performs its mesmerizing *pas de trois*
with gravity and time—as do
all our mutinous monuments. Exquisite
moments of defiance define us—
heirs to Sisyphus,
whose lot, and nature's laws, commit
us to construct and dare anew
with each predestined *denouement*.

Our Hospitality Industry

Facing deindustrialization, northern Appalachia
came to the realization that we had to catch a
new wave. So we've built captivating clusters
of imposing, ultra-modern structures
designed for our redemptive business: hospitality!
Every room in them has its very own facility
featuring the latest in stainless bath décor
among its other catchy features. For your
aesthetic pleasure, windows offer arresting views
of verdant hills and valleys. And if you could use
some quiet space for thought or self-examination,
we offer sound-proof rooms for solitary meditation—
our staff will guide you to sustained reflection
designed to lead your life in a new direction.
Amenities include our dining room, free phone calls,
library, laundry—and 24-hour security, above all.
We've given every thought to our clients' welfare.
We even offer low-cost, on-site wellness care
and useful arts and crafts for your enjoyment.
Thinking of changing careers? Bravo! Employment
opportunities abound on campus!
So do come spend your time with us.
You'll learn metal engraving and furniture making
and earn money doing so. There's no mistaking
our commitment to a better you.
Let us book you: your every need will be tended to.
Both short and long-term stays are available;
we'll make you an offer that's unassailable.
You really can't say no. Our rates are great.
(In fact, they're covered by the state.)

In truth, we mostly value these facilities
for their vast employment opportunities:
in Pennsylvania alone, the industry employs
some twenty thousand people. And our associates enjoy
near-perfect job security. Coal left us high and dry,
but our hospitality industry will never die.

Whitetail Deer

If you meet them, they may hover there
and grant you venture oddly near,
then melt as sylphs into the air—
the lithe and spectral whitetail deer.

I've watched them from my window
as they've leapt an eight-foot fence;
deer don't move so much as flow,
the avatars of elegance.

Who can contemplate a newborn fawn,
then brusquely turn away
unmoved, and not cheer on
the trembling thing to live another day?

Nor is any sight more bittersweet
unless, unknowing, one ignores
the likelihood the darling creature
will not live beyond the age of four.

To miss them not, my wish and call
is this: at night when I'm no longer here
I'll dream of them, but not by day recall
the lithe and spectral whitetail deer.

Gravity Hill

In Pennsylvania, gravity's the law.
But in Bedford wood stands Gravity Hill,
where up goes down and down goes up. In awe
you'll watch cars drift uphill, and water spilled
flow up. There skiers slalom to the top
and then laboriously clamber down.
If this seems too hard to believe, then stop
and see it for yourself. I must allow
that somehow the whole place disorients:
it seems nature has been violated.
And if you still think all this makes no sense,
your suspicion may be vindicated.
    But shall we simply quit the mythical,
    or now and then permit a miracle?

SUMMER

Summer!

Word association: *Summer!*

To students summer spells *vacation*;
to their teachers, *liberation*.
Luckless kids must stay in *school*,
and maybe never hit the *pool*.

Working parents? Their
first thought is always *child care*.
With good reason,
they have doubts about the *season*.

Folks all over mention *sun*;
mostly children think of *fun*.
But hardy grownups bring up *hiking*
or hopping on their bikes and *biking*.

Summer brings no special charm
to those still living on the farm.
With a tanned and rueful smirk,
they'll respond with one word: *work*.

Those confined to the inner city
may be wont to name *humidity*,
or simply bring up summer's *heat*
or teeming dangers on *the street*.

A form of word association is poetry,
lovingly crafted though it be.

Of all the arts most introspective,
it most reflects its author's perspective.
Though his solitary life may spawn a story,
the poet's best work is revelatory—
even if it speaks a truth you always knew,
a verity you've long possessed,
but never knew just why it was true
until you saw it as a poem expressed.

To the Rail Trail

You call me and I come, you grey old lady.
Conceived of robber barons but work of honest hands,
abandoned, now resplendent,
you carry me past rivers, mountains, farms, and fields.

You take me back into the past,
to towns that were, and still are,
transformed like you;
to those who live and those who sleep,
to those who knew you as I would know you.

I heard your burly rhythms
and your klaxons in my youth,
and strain to catch them on the winds,
but hear instead the birds and rushing waters.
Their melodies are lovely to be sure,
but can't you sing, just once more—
      for me?

Yourself, you're not that much to look at now,
outshone by your surroundings;
yet I glide along you in a trance—
Drawn in, Drawn in.
Without you, a summer's day
had might as well appear
as the bleak midwinter.

Your sister 'cross the way
has her fame and fuss and fortune,
her bustle, bells, and commerce,

her pride of place in history—
her sirens call to many.
Yet I come to you and want no other.

These degenerating bones
will ache from tending you,
until they fall on you
as cinders in your Age of Steam.

The Girl at the Railing

Had he only seen her, Norman Rockwell
would have painted the girl at the railing.
Glove on left hand, her ponytail trailing
pertly from her ball cap, our mademoiselle
screamed as her heroes came to bat,
as if her tiny voice, drowned in the roar
of the crowd, guaranteed a winning score.
But what she wanted even more than that,
it seemed—her Holy Grail—was a foul ball.
All winter long, she had plotted her strategy:
two righties pitching meant that a battery
of lefthanded hitters would scatter all
through both teams' lineups—they normally hit
fouls to the third base side! So there she stood,
positioning herself as best she could:
the walk behind the lower seats permitted
her to range along the left field line.
But frame after frame, she met with frustration
as slowly she came to the realization
of one major flaw in her crafty design:
the wayward balls that came her way
sailed over her home team-capped head,
or died in the seats before her, instead.
And yet our heroine never lost faith,
even as odds of prevailing diminished:
she carried herself with unwavering ardor,
cheering and fielding the stands all the harder.
By the ninth inning, her heroes were finished,
as was her souvenir-hunting foray.
How did she feel going home empty-gloved,

let down, twice over, by the team she loved?
I wondered if she'd aged by more than a day
in that park, or whether the experience
had sapped her winsome confidence
that balls would always bounce her way.

The Meadowcroft Rock Shelter

One summer eighteen thousand years ago,
the first Pennsylvanians crept along a creek,
having stalked the elk herd nearly a week—
they didn't speak of weeks back then, though,
just days, or perhaps a quarter moon.
The strong man in the clan pierced an elk's hide
with a spear. (The unfortunate elk was still inside.)
The boys of the clan killed it off with roughhewn
rocks: stone-flaked spear points were too precious
to risk breaking on a dying elk. They stayed
three days beneath a rocky ledge and made
themselves as comfortable as the arduous
conditions of the time allowed. Who were those
wanderers huddled there, five thousand years
before the first known Indians appeared?
Where did they come from? Where did they go?
No one knows. They left their seeds and stones
and plenty of toasted animal bones.
Of themselves they left only their shadows.

Purple Coneflowers

Photo from wallpaperflare.com

Ode to Purple Coneflowers

While hiking in July through heavy wood,
I neared a clearing up ahead, a bright
and sun-filled place. Approaching there, I stood
in awe of what my mind's eye saw: a flight
of levitating purple jellyfish
above a meadow, with an orangish

beanie button crowning each. Or had I
seen a floating flock of purple shuttlecocks,
their rusty noses thrusting toward the sky?
Desiring to resolve this paradox,
I moved on tip-toe to the meadow's edge
and spied a riotous assemblage

of giant cocktail parasols, rejected
by some tiki bar, perhaps, as oversized.
Discarded, their purple blooms erected
over gangly swizzle sticks, those despised
umbrellas, grown to Brobdingnagian
dimensions, filled a strange, a happy and

exotic space. But knowing senses' powers
to deceive, I blinked, and saw before me a
posse of Eastern purple coneflowers,
known to botany as *Echinacea purpurea*.
If *mid-summer's flowers are to spring's*
as one to ten, the king-size color coneflowers bring

to summer surely balances that scale.
And coneflower parts appear in preparations
treating colds, sore throats, infections, ail-
ments of the skin, the flu, and inflammations.
That's a living, finer thing by far
than purple jellyfish, or exiles from a tiki bar.

The Tombstone

*in the Meyers Burial Ground
outside Meyersdale, Pennsylvania*

**Sue J.
Aged 12 ys. & 9 ms. & 6 ds.**

**Clara B.
Aged 9 ys. & 2 ms. & 12 ds.**

Daughters of S.P. and Maggie Meyers

Died June 4, 1891

*Two precious ones from us have gone
The voices we loved are stilled
Their place is vacant in our home,
Which never can be filled*

The girls, sisters, died in a fire.

My People Was Tools

> After Kirk Judd's
> *My People Was Music*

My people was mattocks that scraped the sod
and heaved it up and sectioned the peat
and pried it from the Irish earth,
and wheelbarrows that hauled it,
and shovels that fed it to smoky furnaces.
They was reins and harnesses and saddle blankets
for horses—the ones that were rightly owned
and the ones that were borrowed—
barreed was their word—
if you know what I mean.
My people was long-handled spades
that poked potato holes in the ground
and dug up the potatoes two times a year,
one crop in the summer and one in the winter.
Year after year,
season after season,
cycle after cycle,
spring and fall,
spring and fall.
Till there was no more potatoes
and they come here.

My people was wood and iron grape presses
and vats called *tinos* for making wine in Tuscany
and oaken barrels for keeping the wine.
They was olive presses made of stone,
and casks for storing the olive oil,

and flasks for serving it.
My people was glass-covered hotbeds
for birthing tomato plants,
and sharp-pointed sticks for planting them
and holding them up as they grew,
and baskets for picking them,
and food mills and jars for canning.
They was sickles for harvesting artichokes
and scythes for mowing wheat,
and stones for grinding wheat to flour,
and broomsticks for rolling the flour into pasta.
My people was hatchets for killing chickens
and pots to boil them
and knives for slicing them
and cleavers for butchering pigs.

And when they come to this country,
them that had some use here survived,
and them that didn't disappeared
or went back to the old country;
the grape presses and food mills and canning gear
come and stayed, but the olive crushers went back.
The mattocks give birth to pickaxes,
some with short handles for clawing coal
in coal seams three feet high,
and the candles that lit homes back home
become oil-wick lamps
and carbide lamps on miners' heads.
The long-handled spades evolved
and give birth to square-bladed,
short-shafted shovels for picking up coal;
I still taste coal dust in my mouth.

The rakes that once groomed gardens
reappeared with broad, solid heads
for pulling steaming coke from coke ovens.
Straw baskets that carried lunches
to European fields changed
to dinner pails of steel.

Some of my people went to work on the railroad;
they was lanterns and flares
so engineers could see
what was up ahead or back behind.
And the clickety-clack of those rails
is the beat of my heart.
Some of 'em was crowbars and claw hammers;
they entered the fireboxes of steam locomotives
and tore the fire bricks out of there—
sometimes before the fire was out.
They was buckets for carrying mortar,
and hods for carrying the new bricks,
and trowels to reline the firebox with 'em.
Wrenches used on wagon wheels grew up
as crescent wrenches, or pipe wrenches,
four foot long and heavy as lead.
Some of 'em liberated themselves
from the B&O Railroad and fled to my house
where they still lie oiled
and ready in my garage—
'cause just like anyone I never know
when I might need a four-foot pipe wrench
in my home.

Yep, my people was tools.
And now the tools have morphed
into laptops and smartphones,
operable all by such soft hands.

Joe Zucco's Star Turn

Joe Zucco lost his forearm in the war, see.
So when he come out of the service,
at the end of his right arm was a hook.
Well, he went back to work in the family
business—the Zucco fireworks factory.
But it turned out he couldn't work no more
in the shop—he kep' droppin' explosive
charges. Which scared us employees there.
So his pap give him a job in the office,
which worked out real good 'cause Joe
was left-handed anyhow. He was also
smart and suited to manage. He took
a bookkeepin' class and got real good
at keepin' the family business's books,
usin' just his left hand and his hook.
No business ever had a better accountant—
he kep' 'em books better'n anyone could.
Well, when ol' man Zucco died, Joe and John,
his younger brother, took the business on.
And they, especially Joe, was very competent.
Now, Joe never took a wife. I hoped he would
but he didn't. He lived in a small apartment
about a mile down the winding road
from the plant—no one ever dared
live any closer to it in case it blowed
up. And Joe always took very good care
of hisself. He could shop and he could drive,
he could cook and he could clean—
he had the cleanest place I ever seen.
Once in a while John's wife Claire

would come to the plant and she'd cut
Joe's fingernails. Which never took long
'cause he only had five.
Well, Joe was a most congenial fellow,
a friend t'all. People would stop by
the plant just to talk to that guy.
And ol' Joe he always made
time fer 'em all. Havin' no wife
and kids, he devoted his whole life
to the town of Kimpton. He had a strong
sense of what was right and wrong.
He was the King of the Lions and Moose
—or whatever they call the Moose head.
At the VFW he helped as best he could,
and marched with 'em in every parade
in town. And then he got elected city
treasurer, and that wadn't no pity
vote, neither, 'cause like I said,
ol' Joe was always very good
at keepin' books. And then they made
him the town of Kimpton's mayor.
And he served a record seven terms.
And there was never no use
in runnin' against him, although
no one ever wanted to anyhow—
he done so good at runnin' the town.
There was just one thing, though,
that struck folks as odd about Joe.
The only public place he wouldn't go
was to a funeral—he said he just hated
the thought of someone bein' shut
up in a box forever in the ground.

Mebbe his own brush with mortality
in the service made him somewhat
shy about goin' to the mortuary,
I don' know. Well, anyhow,
when Joe was sixty-seven or eight,
he got sick and couldn't work no more.
He also had to give up bein' mayor.
And then the next year in May,
Joe give up the ghost and died.
And his brother John complied
with Joe's wishes. He felt duty bound
not to put Joe in a box in the ground.
That's when things got complicated.
He obviously had to have Joe cremated.
But the Zuccos was good Catholics, see,
and that particular religion
never did care much for cremation,
although Pope Whoever did say it's okay
sometimes. But the Pope also said
that Catholics got to bury their dead
in a blessed Catholic cemetery.
Which John refused to do with his brother.
(Which seemed kinda silly to me
since Joe was boxed up anyway.
But I guess ya call that brotherly love.)
Well, Father Raines give Joe a funeral
in the church despite there bein' no burial.
Then John had to find some other
place for Joe, so he put him at home above
his fireplace. But Claire found that objectable.
So John put 'im out of sight in the laundry
room. But that seemed awful disrespectable.

So John took his brother down
to the plant one day and there he
set him on a shelf in the office
where Joe rendered such faithful service
to the company and also run the town.
But then people'd come in and talk
and make jokes about that box—
"John, how's your brother today?"
and "I come to see the mayor."
Stuff like that. Well, John let people know
that he didn't appreciate the humor
in that when it come to ol' Joe.
So one Sundy near the end of June,
when he had the factory all to hisself,
John found the most opportune
moment to take Joe off the shelf.
He carefully divvied Joe up
in three parts, and laid him lengthways
in each of three colored stages
of a rocket, so the thing would go up
straight in the air and blow up
like normal. And then on the 4th of July,
Joe made his final appearance
in the sky over town, at a height
o' 300 feet. The first phase
of the rocket was red, the second white,
and the third burst was blue.
And when that incandescence
lit up that nighttime sky,
you never seen a more touching sight.
Every single person thereabouts—
every man, woman, and child that gazed

up at them bursts and the evanescence
fallin' all around 'em through the air—
they was cryin' and rubbin' their eyes
and tryin' to wipe away tears
like they never done in other years.
I thought that musta been due
to thoughts o' Joe not bein' there.
Then later on I learned the truth
about Joe Zucco's final whereabouts.
Speakin' o' which, by now most o' Joe
is probly all the way down the Ohio
and the Mississippi to the Gulf o' Mexico.
But as you know, it's truly been said
that even after they die the dead
live on in all of us.
And it's a true fact that in anyone
that's still alive today
there's a molecule of everyone
that's ever lived—Caesar, Columbus,
Elvis and Jesus and JFK.
And I guess we got more of ol' Joe
inside of us than other people might,
at least us that seen the fireworks that night.

Photo by Jingda Chen

The Confederate Graveyard
Near Cumberland, Maryland

While hiking on a summer's day, I spied
a flag-bedecked enclosure off a short
way from my path. My curiosity
aroused, I found a cemetery there.
Confederate and U.S. flags flew high
above the graves of James and Sallie Pollock.
James, who fought for Dixie in the cavalry,
was taken prisoner at Gettysburg.
His sister Sallie was arrested as
a Southern spy who carried letters meant
for Jefferson Davis and General Lee.
The Cumberland Historic Cemetery
group has placed a sign there: James and Sallie,
we are told, were fervent "freedom fighters
that upheld the Christian Cross."

A foreigner might think it odd to find
a graveyard decked with those entangled, spangled
banners: soldiers fighting under them killed half
a million of each other, and they maimed
a million more. Did they not perceive some
difference, some principle worth fighting for?
James's stone dispels the puzzle thusly:
he enlisted only in "The War for States' Rights."
The foreigner might ask, "Such as? Whose rights?
What rights belong to states and not humanity?"

POSTED

PRIVATE PROPERTY
GET OUT
NOW
THIS MEANS YOU

NO SITTING, STANDING,
STOPPING OR STAYING
NO BIKING, BATHING
OR BUTTERFLY WATCHING
NO CAMPING, CANOEING
OR CUTTING OF FIREWOOD
IN CASE OF SOLAR ECLIPSE,
NO STARGAZING!

NO HUNTING, FISHING, TRAPPING
OR OTHER SENSELESS CRUELTY
TO ANIMALS

EXCEPT BY OWNER

VIOLATORS WILL BE PROSECUTED

**Ordering Grits
in Culpeper, Virginia**

Some years back while touring the South—
specifically, the Old Dominion—
I thought I'd do as natives do
and put some Southern food in my mouth,
just like any proper Virginian.

One fateful morn I left my room,
feeling oddly miscast
in that Southern milieu,
and went to the dining room set to consume
my first-ever Southern breakfast repast.

There a red-haired waitress named Faye
gave me a menu for me to peruse
as she "fetched" me some biscuits I didn't request.
When she returned, not knowing what I should say,
I blurted, "Faye, it's the 'Creamy Grits' that I choose."

Pleased with my judicious selection,
and having kept my wits
about me as a good Northern guest,
I calmly awaited my scrumptious confection
of true Southern grits.

When the grits arrived I received quite a fright,
for in them was something yellow and icky.
At first I just sat there in Yankee vexation.
I wished to do nothing that seemed impolite,
but didn't want grits that were yellow and sticky.

"Faye," I finally managed to sputter,
"what is this yellowish goop in my food?"
Looking perplexed, she gave this explanation:
"Why honey, that's nothin' but butter,"
displaying a kind and concerned attitude.

"Thanks," I replied, "but I'd wanted some milk
on my grits—to eat them like oatmeal."
Faye paused and then, with some hesitation,
said that on grits they'd never put things of that ilk,
seeming to find my suggestion surreal.

But seeing that I was set in my preference,
Faye suggested I stand by a window,
look in the kitchen, ask the head cook
for the alien milk, and thence
I'd return to my breakfast tableau.

I really thought that she ought to get it,
but seeking not to be uncouth,
I decided I would overlook
her nonchalance and let it
go, and rose from my booth

to get the damn milk. Then I stood
where she said for quite a long while,
not quite suppressing a rising displeasure
and waiting about as long as I could,
resisting a growing level of bile.

When the chef finally showed,
he gave me the milk as soon as he was able,
not knowing, I guess, why I wanted that treasure.
Then came the worst of the whole episode:
when I returned, Faye had cleared off my table.

Yes, the entire table was bald—
gone were grits and biscuits and all.
Faye came to the table as soon as I called.
"Faye, you cleared off my table!" I bawled.
"We thought yuh-awl was duh-un," she drawled.

"No, I wasn't done," I fumed.
"But now I am, and don't you dare"
—I declared in a huff—
"charge this meal to my room,"
and left to have my breakfast elsewhere.

At first I thought you'd plainly see
that all throughout I acted right;
my feelings wound up ruffled
after all became a travesty
my virtue helped incite.

But then I asked what went awry.
Did Faye or I beget contention
in this wee kerfuffle?
Do you see a good or bad guy,
or just misapprehension?

In any case, I'll tell you this
as long as fate permits:
when you wander try new stuff—
adventures you don't want to miss.
But don't ever order grits.

EPILOGUE

MICHAEL COMISKEY

Pittsburgh

The city America's made of
resembles a model train display—
riven by rivers, ravines, and vertiginous
hills, stitched by ten tunnels and 446 bridges.
Hell with the lid off in Dickens' day—
and long after that—land of fire and flood,
it's a hard place that its people love.

And since you've asked, we're African, Jewish,
Slovak and Muslim. We've come in waves
from everywhere—Germans, Hungarians, Asians
of eastern and western persuasions.
And we haven't forgotten the old ways—
nope, not the Italians or the Polish.
Did I mention that we're also Irish?

San Francisco has cable cars and windy seas
and streets that sometimes have steps
on the side. Pittsburgh has steps that sometimes
have streets in the center—they climb
hills too steep for streets. And bluffs too steep
for streets or stairs. Here, one sees
cable cars hoisted up vertices

with ropes of steel. Chicago has Lake
Michigan, downtown a famous skyline,
the Navy Pier and Centennial Wheel—
and shoulders big from lifting Pittsburgh steel.
The food is great, the pizza's really fine,

but the place is *flatter than a pancake*—
not like here, where hills and gorges make

for cozy neighborhoods. In almost every city
charms reside, whether large or small in size.
New York has *Le Boucherie* and *coq au vin*.
Here we've got Primanti's, and that's better than
anything they've got, and don't tell us otherwise.
Boston has its harbor and its history.
But it's not home to me.

Pittsburgh, you're afflicted now with banes
that even your considerable brains and sinews
cannot cure. The slaughter of the innocents
you've known, and the daily hail of violence:
Shotspotter anchors the nightly news.
The races race, and live, in different lanes;
your often somber skies dump punishing rains

that liquefy your hills. The yawning separation
of the many and the few divides you
as no undergirded bridge of steel could span.
If it takes a town to raise a child, can
cities survive these daunting new
times without the care and effort of the nation?
Pittsburgh strives, awaiting that determination.

Acknowledgments

The poems "Forgotten Places," "The Cash King," "To the Rail Trail," "Birth Waters" and "Monongahela Valley" have appeared in *The Loyalhanna Review*. "Fallingwater" has appeared in *Pennsylvania's Poetic Voices*. "I Live Alone" has appeared in *Rune*. "Shanksville," "The Maple Trees," and "The Meadowcroft Rock Shelter" have appeared in *Prize Poems 2023* (Pennsylvania Poetry Society, Inc.)

Hanna Fox of Princeton, New Jersey has made these poems better. She is the tough but fair and amiable critic every poet should have.

I owe a special debt to Dr. Beverly Peterson of The Pennsylvania State University and The College of William and Mary for her much cherished friendship, patient tutoring, and unfailing encouragement of my writing.